*To Every Thing
There Is a Season*

To Every Thing There Is a Season

H. A. Hopgood

RESOURCE *Publications* • Eugene, Oregon

TO EVERY THING THERE IS A SEASON

Copyright © 2022 H. A. Hopgood. All rights reserved. Except for brief quotations in critical publications or reviews, no part of this book may be reproduced in any manner without prior written permission from the publisher. Write: Permissions, Wipf and Stock Publishers, 199 W. 8th Ave., Suite 3, Eugene, OR 97401.

Resource Publications
An Imprint of Wipf and Stock Publishers
199 W. 8th Ave., Suite 3
Eugene, OR 97401

www.wipfandstock.com

PAPERBACK ISBN: 978-1-6667-3233-7
HARDCOVER ISBN: 978-1-6667-2591-9
EBOOK ISBN: 978-1-6667-2592-6

JUNE 11, 2024 5:21 AM

Contents

Acknowledgements | ix

Introduction | xi

❧ Spring ☙

Spring in the Valley | 3
Commandment of Love | 4
Grace for Grace | 5
"Yea, Lord" | 6
Love Wears Small Shoes | 7
One Cherry Tree | 8
By the Green of the Trees | 9
United in God | 10
Divine Plans | 11
Divine Drinks | 12
Darkness Scene | 13
Aceldama | 14
Interpreting the Cross | 15
In Manus Tuas | 16
God Changes the Times | 17
The Road to Emmaus | 18
The Sheep's Confession | 19

Psalm 23 | 21
Let Us Go On | 23
Call Me | 24

⋐ Summer ⋑

The Lord's Day Forest | 29
The Dandelion | 30
The Unity of God | 31
Knowing God | 32
God's Will Is Perfect | 33
Sea-wave (or Self-Expression) | 34
Hills of Help | 35
The Killdeer | 36
"Our Soul Is Dried Away" | 37
Olive Branches | 38

⋐ Autumn ⋑

Seasonal Clothes | 41
Bread and Wine | 42
Reformationtag | 43
Carbonado (or Life's Journey) | 44
From Mourning to Morning | 45
Elizabeth of Hungary | 46
Will Reunited | 47
Litany of Thanks | 48
Thanksgiving Day | 49
Returning Thanks | 50
How to Be Thankful | 51
Stir Up Thy Church, O Lord | 52

❧ Winter ☙

Cry of the Gull | 55
The Stone | 56
Empty Sea | 57
The Incarnation | 58
The Animals' Eyes | 59
Peace of Paradise | 60
How Many Were There? | 61
Nature's Cosmetic | 62
A Star and a Book | 63
The Revelation | 64

Alphabetical Index | 65

Topical Index | 67

Acknowledgements

I AM GRATEFUL to Elizabeth Hopgood, D.Min.; and Stephanie K. Hopgood, Doctoral Candidate; for their detailed review and excellent suggestions for improving the poetic quality as well as the clarity of these poems.

Introduction

SCRIPTURE AND NATURE are inexhaustible springs of poetic inspiration. Only the divinely inspired poets of the Psalms and Prophets have done justice to these great themes, but countless poets through the ages have obtained joy from exploring their depths. From these two springs, the greater spring of Scripture and the lesser spring of Nature, has come the primary inspiration for the poems in this collection.

This poetry also reflects how Christians express the truths of Scripture in celebrations throughout the year. Like the feasts Israel observed in the Old Testament, Christian holidays come at fixed times in the physical year, using what is available at that particular season to demonstrate and remember God's work of redemption. These celebrations therefore praise the Lord always (every year) and at all times (at each season). That is why poems about Christian holidays remain connected to Scripture and Nature, the two great springs of poetic inspiration. The thoughts that I have dipped into their flow are a little cup I now offer to you.

Spring

SPRING IN THE VALLEY

(For Grandma)

It's Spring in the valley.
(Almost Spring in the mountains!)
The sheep have had their lambs;
Now the elk have calves.

It's Spring in the valley.
(Almost Spring in the mountains!)
There's frost among the tulips
But light snow on peaks.

It's Spring in the valley.
(Almost Spring in the mountains!)
The farmers plow their fields,
While the swans fly north.

COMMANDMENT OF LOVE

Even when inconvenient,
Lord, give me grace
Eternal love
In time and space
To prove thy commandment.

GRACE FOR GRACE

My straightened soul expand
To love and, loving,
Thus to understand
Both myself and thee.
From love to love lead on
As by the hand
A father leads a child.
Alone I cannot stand
Except by love upheld.
By grace I'll not withstand
Thy grace: I'll love by love
That first thou didst impart
And then inspire.

"YEA, LORD"

"Yea, Lord," answered trusting Martha
When Christ asked if she believed
That he was the Resurrection
And the Truth and Life indeed.
She with confidence responded
Through her sorrow, grief, and tears,
"Yea, I know thou art Messiah
And that God will hear thy prayers."

Though we may not ever fully
Understand the works God does,
We can trust that he will only
Do what's best for those he loves.
His great mercy's ever changeless;
He will hear our sighing prayers.
We can rest upon his promise
Reassured that Jesus cares.

May we always be like Martha
When we cannot see ahead,
Not to criticize the Savior
But assert our faith instead.
Even when life's at its darkest
And great grief drags out our days,
Hope in Christ will give us courage
Still in sorrow to sing praise.

LOVE WEARS SMALL SHOES

(To my mother)

Love wears small shoes.
We ask in places,
"How could it fit
In such small spaces?"

Love wears hard shoes.
We learn to say
At clatter's fuss,
"Love comes this way."

Love wears soft shoes.
It does and goes
When oft the served
One never knows.

Love's sturdy shoes
Keep always going.
To learn to wear them
Is well worth knowing.

ONE CHERRY TREE

Midst the bracken and broken
Old stalks of young trees
In the jumble of tangled
Bare limbs before leaves,
One cherry tree blossomed.

BY THE GREEN OF THE TREES

By the green of the trees
    Quiet comes
Thoughts ordered run
The heart finds ease
By the green of the trees

By the green of the trees
    Quiet stands
We hold God's hand
Frustration flees
By the green of the trees

By the green of the trees
    Quiet hears
We know Jesus near
And on his knees
Underneath the green trees

UNITED IN GOD

Faithful Creator
And Merciful Judge,
Lord of our nature,
We pray thee to pledge
To be what thou art;
Since as thou'rt inclined
In the thought of our heart
T'ward us, we find.
Yet as thou art
In thyself thou wilt be
To those who depart
From conceptions of thee
By unbelief blighted:
Truths we falsely divide
May we find reunited
In the wound in thy side.

DIVINE PLANS

God made the natural world:
He ordered out its days.
God made the universe
Designed to give him praise;
But before he made man,
He had in mind
    Salvation's plan.

God made the heavens high:
He ordered all things well.
God made the angels bright
But condemned some when they fell.
Thus was hell now a place
And added soon
    A fallen race.

Christ came to earth for man
Despite what he had seen.
Christ died for sinful man
That he might man redeem.
He brought down to man
What was his first
    Creation plan.

DIVINE DRINKS

The pagan gods continual nectar drink,
And Jollity among them reigns as king.
These waft within an ever-budding Spring,
Found lounging by the stream of pleasure's brink
In which, like sweet oblivion, troubles sink;
While their devotees daily worship bring
As bribes for help in some occasional thing.
Indifference like theirs we ought not think
Comparable to thy true nature, Lord.
As if thou wouldest make a mark more sure
Of who is God and what are thoughts divine,
Thou didst a work such gods could not afford
By choosing gall beyond what men endure
That through thy suff'rings we might drink of wine.

DARKNESS SCENE

As the noontide dark spread o'er the cross,
It brought a certain terror
To those who found the sun's soon loss
A single source of horror.
While their darkness came to light,
As in a mirror,
Thickness of their evil eye,
Their blindness, showed e'en clearer.
But those whose sight was marred by grief
Could find out nothing better
That could give both eye and heart relief
Than darkness that the scene would cover.

ACELDAMA

Aceldama, the field of blood,
    The stranger's final place,
    The alien's long home,
Expedient for outcast dead.

Aceldama, the field of blood,
    Potter's promised purchase
    By Israel's good sum
As falsely spent as falsely made.

Aceldama, the field of blood,
    Most unkind charity
    Of bold hypocrisy
Scorns Christ and strangers, loved of God.

Aceldama, the field of blood,
    The gathered outcasts' rest
    (*Lo-ammi* now beloved)
Christ Jesus bought them by his blood.

INTERPRETING THE CROSS

Christ victorious,
Christ all-glorious,
Is in the cross now seen.

IN MANUS TUAS

Into thy hands
I commend my spirit,
Into hands that hold
My soul in life
For thou hast made
Both for a purpose.

Into thy hands
I commend my spirit,
Into piercéd hands
Giv'n for my life
By the last Man,
The Quick'ning Spirit.

GOD CHANGES THE TIMES

O glorious Resurrection Day!
O blessed First-day Morn!
What changes have been underway
E'er this third day was born!

Three days ago the angry crowd
Rejoiced with bitter scorn;
The saints now shout with joy aloud,
While Death and Darkness mourn.

Jews sealed the tomb, Rome mounted guard
As ev'ning drew to night.
But angel legions kept the ward,
When Christ rose in his might.

THE ROAD TO EMMAUS

As gilds the sun the glowing West,
No farther go, but be our Guest.
Not alone the Law commands
But thy gracious words commend
Themselves and thee that so
We can let neither go.

By entertaining we requite
The One whom we constrain tonight
To dwell within our poor abode.
Since hope surprised us on the road,
Our burning hearts now feel
Thou art our only weal.

The weal of woeful hearts and blind
Before thou opened up our mind
To understand the ancient word
Of Moses, which we'd always heard
But knew not when or how
They'd be fulfilled till now.

Fulfilled before our very eyes!
No measure for our great surprise
But 'change for greater awe instead,
When we know Christ in breaking bread.
Although the bread remains,
The incrusted Word sustains.

THE SHEEP'S CONFESSION[*]

(Psalm 23)

My Shepherd is the LORD;
Ne'er want shall I.
Green pastures he'll afford
In which to lie.

Beside the waters still
He'll lead my soul,
By means of which he will
Restore it whole.

The paths of righteousness
He'll lead me in,
And there direct my steps
For his own name.

E'en though I walk the vale
Through shadows dark
Of death, I'll fear no ill;
With me thou art.

Thy shepherd's rod and staff
My comfort are.
Thou wilt on my behalf
A place prepare,

---

[*] This is a metrical translation from the original Hebrew by the author.

A place to eat in sight
Of hateful foes.
My head with oil anoint;
My cup o'erflows.

Sure good and mercy shall
My footsteps chase;
And in God's house I'll dwell
For endless days.

PSALM 23*

The LORD my Shepherd is
Ne'er want shall I.
In pastures green
He makes me lie:
The waters still
He leads me by;
My soul he does restore.
He leads me in
The righteous paths
For his own name.
E'en though I walk
Within the vale
Of death with shadows dark
I'll fear no ill;
For you're with me
Your rod and staff
Do comfort me.
On my behalf
A table you prepare
Before men's sight
Who wish me war.
You will anoint
My head with oil;
My cup flows o'er.

---

* This is a poetical translation from the original Hebrew by the author.

The good, it's very true,
And mercy shall
My soul pursue
Through all life's days;
And I'll dwell in
God's house always.

LET US GO ON

(Hebrews 6:1-8)

Let us go on
    Unto perfection,
Not laying again
    The old foundation
Of repentance from dead works
And the sin that daily lurks
    Within our evil hearts.

CALL ME

Call me
When the merry earth listens
To the minstrel bird singing
To the leafy castanets.
When the tiny flower's silent music making,
Call me.

Call me
When the weary earth listens
To the long-awaited rains
To sigh with her relief and joy.
When the wee tree frog renews his song,
Call me.

Call me
When the softened earth listens
To the stormy winds roaring
To the pounding of the rain.
When the tow'ring fir trees stoop and bend,
Call me.

Call me
When the quiet earth listens
To the nearly silent snow falling
To still all other sounds.
When all the world's a wonder,
Call me.

Call me
When your waking soul listens
To the beauty and the aid that's giv'n
To us and all creation.
When for prayer and praise you're ready,
Call me.

Summer

THE LORD'S DAY FOREST

A thousand spires
    point to heaven.
Ten thousand hands
    wave praise to God.
A hundred thousand
    gentle voices
In chorus sing,
    "God reigns above."

THE DANDELION

In France its golden face
Is taken to compare
The ladies' looks and grace
And complement the fair.
But here it is replaced
With grass in lawn repair.

In France the flow'r enjoys
An honorable name
By florists all employed,
But here another fame
Of "weed" and "child's toy,"
Yet smiles just the same.

THE UNITY OF GOD

God's will is one
With his love and his goodness.
If we would try
To divide them, we miss.

Holiness crowns
Both God's works and his thought,
Since it pervades
All his being as God.

KNOWING GOD

Disciples never choose the Lord,
    Nor can one know the Son;
But those the Father gave to him
    And by the Father drawn.

No one can God the Father know,
    None to the Father come,
Except he be revealed to him
    By the begotten Son.

The Holy Spirit testifies
    And speaks not of his own
But points to Christ in whom we see
    The Godhead all in One.

GOD'S WILL IS PERFECT

God's will is perfect
Beyond understanding
To earthlies as we are,
Created from dust;

Changeless, eternal,
Including repentance
By One without turning
Or shadow thereof.

Justice, compassion,
With wrath and longsuff'ring
Are meted together,
Proportioned divine.

SEA-WAVE (OR SELF-EXPRESSION)

A sea-wave rose;
On the edge
At the fringe
Of the sea, it rose.
Drawn up by the moon, it rose.
Borne up by the wind, it rose.
Pulled down by the earth, still it rose;
Till the earth rose.
To it the wave extended itself,
To it the wave expressed itself,
On it the wave expended itself
And fled finished into the sea.
Brother wave took the place of it,
As it slipped back into the sea.
Other waves took what was left of it
And swallowed it into the sea.
Yet the earth showed
What the sea had done
Wave upon wave upon wave.
Of the sand and the spume
That the wave had flung,
Only was left
What matched the sea.

HILLS OF HELP*

(Psalm 121)

I'll lift mine eyes unto the hills
From whence my help doth come:
My help comes from the LORD who hath
Made both the earth and heav'n.

He'll never let thy foot be mov'd,
Nor slumbers he who keeps
His Israel. Behold, he's prov'd
He slumbers not, nor sleeps.

The LORD's thy keeper; he's thy shade
Upon thy right-hand side.
The sun shall not thee smite by day
Nor moon at eventide.

The LORD from evil shall defend;
He will preserve thy soul,
Thy going out and coming in
From now through ages all.

---

* This is a metrical translation from the original Hebrew by the author.

THE KILLDEER

A killdeer cries,
He cries, she cries,
While others a-bed.
More runs than flies
From the ocean's edge,
From my booted tread.

"OUR SOUL IS DRIED AWAY"

Seeking things of flesh
To satisfy their lust,
Israel to Moses wept,
"Our soul is dried away."

"Egypt's flesh-pots full
And gardens fresh we ate.
Now this manna light we loathe —
Our soul is dried away."

When we could be fed
With Christ the Living Bread,
Do we often cry instead,
"Our soul is dried away"?

OLIVE BRANCHES

An olive tree of goodly stock
    With wild branch is seen,
But lying stricken on the ground,
    The branch that there had been.

Though cast aside, it's yet reserved,
    Nor gathered to be burned:
The Husbandman again takes up
    The branch he once had spurned.

He grafts it in where none had been,
    And now the tree has more
With which to give and glory in
    Than could have been before.

Autumn

SEASONAL CLOTHES

Red and orange leaves
Robe the oak and maple trees
As autumn unfolds.

BREAD AND WINE

As many grains one loaf its shape will give,
Thus true believers are Christ's body made
With each supported by the flesh he gave;
And still he gives that, as he lives, they live.
By faith his blood becomes our sacred wine,
Which will our stricken spirits yet restore;
And we as branches will bear fruit and more,
Abiding, husbanded, within the Vine.
Hear Wisdom praying us her wine to taste:
She standing at the city's gates will call.
Yet we must seek her at her gate and wall.
O grant us, Christ, that by thy Spirit's grace,
Partaking of the Sacrifice may we
The living sacrifices also be.

REFORMATIONTAG

While kids to costumes wild were changing
And neighbors tricks or treats exchanging,
Never reveler came ranging
From the silent house on the corner.

On that most lawless of all nights,
The strong wind bobbed no colorful lights
Nor struck nor strewed any cutesy frights
From the sober house on the corner.

Throughout the day no sign of life was seen;
The ev'ning windows held no hopeful gleam,
Nor issued any sound of Halloween
From the boring house on the corner.

However, it may have perchance been said
The smell of sausage and of gingerbread
Across the night the strong wind swirled and spread
From the merry house on the corner.

What need have they of costumes, lights, or fog,
Of yowling cat or some old creaking log
To keep their *Reformationtag*
In the happy house on the corner?

CARBONADO (OR LIFE'S JOURNEY)

Be patient with me.
The river is fast.
This log shakes and bends;
Though not first nor last,
   Yet I'm
      Afraid
         Of falling.

Be patient with me
By the waterfall's edge.
It's beautiful here
By the unguarded ledge,
   But I'm
      Afraid of
         Falling.

Be patient with me.
The trail is long,
The path often steep.
I'm not always strong,
   And I'm afraid
      Of
         Falling.

You've been patient with me.
Our dangers are past.
We came safely through
And, home now at last,
No more need I fear falling.

FROM MOURNING TO MORNING

From mourning to morning
Is only a night.
The hours in between though,
That shut out the light,
May be more than twelve.
Our night may be shorter
If God so deem best:
Whatever the length is,
With joy will come rest.
Our night, when it's with us,
Seems endless and cold,
While even the promise,
Though precious as gold,
Rings dull but for faith.

ELIZABETH OF HUNGARY

(To my mother)

In emulating Christ
She edifies Christians.

Her love of virtue
(Hearty as bread)
    Angered the wicked,
    Inspired the wise,
    Encouraged the weary.

Her valor of charity
(Sweet as roses)
    Persevered through life,
    Endured through death,
    Remains for ever.

WILL REUNITED

"'Tis done." The final word is giv'n
From him that sits upon the throne.
What word remains in earth or heav'n
Once God himself has said, "'Tis done"?

"Amen," the six-winged seraph answers;
And all creation says, "Amen"
Together in that self-same answer —
The rocks and beasts, as well as men.

Yet with that word all wills created
Assenting with their Lord combine,
While sin and hell withdraw defeated
To fade into the dusk of time.

LITANY OF THANKS

Thank you for your help each day,
Guiding us into your way,
Drawing out our hearts to pray:
    Hear us, holy Jesus.

Thank you for your strength and grace
Patiently to run our race,
Seeking thus your steps to trace:
    Hear us, holy Jesus.

Thank you that you intercede.
God with God for us now plead;
Bold we come to you in need:
    Hear us, holy Jesus.

Thank you for what you have planned,
Placing us at your right hand.
To our help your hosts command:
    Hear us, holy Jesus.

THANKSGIVING DAY

On this day above the rest,
Think how our Creator blest
Grants us more than full
Gifts for body as for soul.

Holy day we name it now.
Heart prepare with mind to bow:
Bring your highest praise
Into courts of heav'n to raise.

Let today's inspired lays
Sanctify the other days.
May we not forget
All his daily benefits.

RETURNING THANKS

Thanks for all you do each day
To keep me as I live,
For all the sins you wash away,
For all the grace you give.

Thanks for daily drawing near
To teach what I should know —
Discretion, wisdom, knowledge, fear —
To show me where to go.

Thanks for all you take away,
For mem'ries that remain
Of the delights of former days
That made me who I am.

Thanks for showing who you are
The only Trinity;
Exalted, holy, gracious, pure,
Love for eternity.

HOW TO BE THANKFUL[*]

(Psalm 100)

Rejoice aloud before the LORD
All peoples of the earth:
With gladness serve him; also come
Before his face with mirth.

Know in yourselves the LORD is God,
The only God he is.
He is the one who us has made,
Nor did we make ourselves.

We are his people and his sheep
Who in his pastures graze.
Come with thanksgiving through his gates,
Into his courts with praise.

To him be thankful; bless his name,
E'en for the LORD is good:
His mercy and his truth shall stand
Fore'er as they have stood.

[*] This is a metrical translation from the original Hebrew by the author.

STIR UP THY CHURCH, O LORD

Stir up thy church, O Lord,
And bear her on thy wing.
So give to her that what thou seek'st
Shall be what she will bring.

Stir up thy church, O Lord;
Direct thy people's ways
That they may walk within the path
Of mercy, truth, and grace.

Stir up thy church, O Lord;
Arouse her in this night.
May she so strive that through thy Son
She e'er may dwell in Light.

Stir up thy church, O Lord;
May thy wise Spirit move
On thy belov'd that thy good will
As perfect they may prove.

O Father who hast giv'n
The church to thine own Son;
With thy good Spirit seal to them
The vict'ry he hath won.

Winter

CRY OF THE GULL

The cry of the gull
Is the life of the sea,
As lonely a call
As it's thought to be.
The wildest shore
Is feared less dull
If above the surf's roar
Comes the cry of a gull.

THE STONE

      the stone   the stone
The Stone rejected   the same is become
         rejected the stone

    the stone
the stone   the head
          the head-stone

   the corner-stone
of the corner   the Stone
   chief corner-stone

    This is the Stone   the Lord's stone
This   is   the Lord's doing,
   this stone,   this Stone the Lord,

                           our stone
and it is marvelous in our eyes.
                 it is marvelous

EMPTY SEA

The sky is grey,
The sea is green.
For fourteen miles
There's nothing between
Those two colors.

THE INCARNATION

Christ took unto his Godhead
What had not been before,
All that is our manhood,
Now his forevermore.

The Word before creation
God with his Father is;
Now, mysterious relation,
He's Brother in our flesh.

THE ANIMALS' EYES

The almond-shaped eyes of oxen wise
Are wide with wonder, yet not rimm'd with white.
As also from the manger, Uncreated Light
Shines softly on the sheep's square-center'd eyes.
From gloomy rafters low o'erhead, the dove
Peers down with tiny bits of polished glass.
Below, the dusty lashes of the ass
Afford no cover to brown pools of love.
From by the door the cat's unblinking stare
Ought none call common, neither judge as ill.
The Devil finds no place or idle will
In any of the sev'ral natures here.
At such a sight let each man say with me,
"O great and wondrous sacred mystery!"

PEACE OF PARADISE

When the shepherds found the place
And reverently approached,
Suddenly surrounded with
Primeval peace of Paradise,
Once more Man heard God's voice.

HOW MANY WERE THERE?

How many cities were there?
    In Judah great Jerusalem
    But the least small Bethlehem.

How many rooms were there?
    In the inn were none
    But in the stable one.

How many lambs were there?
    Thousands in offering accepted
    But only One perfected.

How many angels were there?
    Where at first one stood,
    Suddenly a multitude.

How many stars were there?
    More than any man knows
    But only one that moves.

How many kings were there?
    One of the worst, three of the best,
    But above all the Greatest.

NATURE'S COSMETIC

The snow makes pretty things look beautiful
And ugly things look not so bad.

A STAR AND A BOOK

Was it only a star?
Was that all it took
To bring kings this far?
A new light's bright look
Brought men of the palaces
To hazard the rocks
And dirty places
To the den of the Fox?
O'er more than Bethlehem's fields,
All comforts forsook —
What great power wields?
Both a star and a Book.

THE REVELATION

"A sword shall pierce
    Thy soul," we hear
In temple grand
    From agéd seer.
Words very true,
    Yet words to fear.

"One woe is past,
    Another comes."
Her man-child born
    To desert runs,
Or flies. She births
    To lose her Son.

In travail cries
    But, sorrows cast,
In joy forgets
    Her anguish past;
For man is born
    And saved at last.

Alphabetical Index

Aceldama, 14
The Animals' Eyes, 59

Bread and Wine, 42
By the Green of the Trees, 9

Call Me, 24
Carbonado (or Life's
    Journey), 44
Commandment of Love, 4
Cry of the Gull, 55

The Dandelion, 30
Darkness Scene, 13
Divine Drinks, 12
Divine Plans, 11

Elizabeth of Hungary, 46
Empty Sea, 57

From Mourning to Morning, 45

God Changes the Times, 17
God's Will Is Perfect, 33
Grace for Grace, 5

Hills of Help, 35
How Many Were There?, 61

How to Be Thankful, 51

In Manus Tuas, 16
The Incarnation, 58
Interpreting the Cross, 15

The Killdeer, 36
Knowing God, 32

Let Us Go On, 23
Litany of Thanks, 48
The Lord's Day Forest, 29
Love Wears Small Shoes, 7

Nature's Cosmetic, 62

Olive Branches, 38
One Cherry Tree, 8
"Our Soul Is Dried Away", 37

Peace of Paradise, 60
Psalm 23, 21

Reformationtag, 43
Returning Thanks, 50
The Revelation, 64
The Road to Emmaus, 18

Seasonal Clothes, 41

Alphabetical Index

Sea-wave (or Self-Expression), 34
The Sheep's Confession, 19
Spring in the Valley, 3
A Star and a Book, 63
Stir Up Thy Church, O Lord, 52
The Stone, 56

Thanksgiving Day, 49

United in God, 10
The Unity of God, 31

Will Reunited, 47

"Yea, Lord", 6

Topical Index

Christian life

Carbonado (or Life's Journey), 44
Elizabeth of Hungary, 46
From Mourning to Morning, 45
In Manus Tuas, 16
Knowing God, 32
"Our Soul Is Dried Away", 37
Stir Up Thy Church, O Lord, 52
"Yea, Lord", 6

Christmas

The Animals' Eyes, 59
How Many Were There?, 61
The Incarnation, 58
Peace of Paradise, 60
The Revelation, 64
A Star and a Book, 63

Communion, the Lord's Supper

Bread and Wine, 42
Divine Drinks, 12
The Road to Emmaus, 18

The Cross, the Crucifixion

Aceldama, 14
Darkness Scene, 13
Interpreting the Cross, 15

Easter, Resurrection

God Changes the Times, 17
The Road to Emmaus, 18
"Yea, Lord", 6

God's nature

God's Will Is Perfect, 33
United in God, 10
The Unity of God, 31

Lord's Supper. See Communion.

Love

Commandment of Love, 4
Grace for Grace, 5
Love Wears Small Shoes, 7

Poems from Scripture

Hills of Help, 35

Topical Index

(Poems from Scripture contiued)
How to Be Thankful, 51
Let Us Go On, 23
Psalm 23, 21
The Sheep's Confession, 19

Redemption

Aceldama, 14
Divine Drinks, 12
Divine Plans, 11
Olive Branches, 38
The Stone, 56
Will Reunited, 47

Resurrection. See Easter.

Sea, Sea-birds

Cry of the Gull, 55

Empty Sea, 57
The Killdeer, 36
Sea-wave (or Self-
    Expression), 34

Thanksgiving

How to Be Thankful, 51
Litany of Thanks, 48
Returning Thanks, 50
Thanksgiving Day, 49

Trees

By the Green of the Trees, 9
Call Me, 24
The Lord's Day Forest, 29
Olive Branches, 38
One Cherry Tree, 8
Seasonal Clothes, 41

www.ingramcontent.com/pod-product-compliance
Lightning Source LLC
Chambersburg PA
CBHW071740040426
42446CB00012B/2415